Sailing Knots

10 Nautical knots you need to know

Alexander Meyer

Text: Alexander Meyer
Illustration: Iris Schorn - @SchornEE

ISBN-10: 1544118198
ISBN-13: 978-1544118192

Content:

Introduction

Sailing knots are a fundamental part of a sailing course and of the skipper exam, because on a boat there is always a line that has to be tied somewhere. Or lines have to be tied to each other. For every situation there is a perfectly secure knot, one that is easy to tie and easy to loosen. I will now explain the most important sailor's knots in word and illustrations. And there are videos about each knot on the Internet for you. You will find the links in the respective chapter.

The following knots are explained:
Figure-eight knot
Square knot
Bowline knot
Cleat knot
Clove hitch
Sheet bend
Double Sheet bend
Round turn and two half hitches
Rolling hitch
Cleat with bowline knot

So let's start:

Figure-eight Knot

In this chapter I show how to tie the figure-eight knot. The figure-eight knot prevents that a line slides out of a pulley or a grommet when the knot is tied at the very end of the line. Follow these steps for tying the figure-eight knot:

I put the line in my left hand. I take the tail with my right hand and place it over the line so that both parts cross.

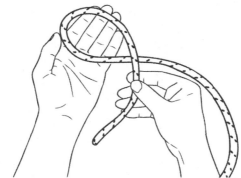

As a result there is now a loop at the end of the line.

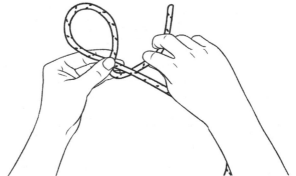

I take the point where the both parts of the line cross each other between my thumb and my forefinger of the left hand.

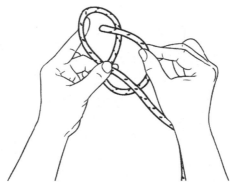

With the right hand I grab the tail underneath the loop. I take it up to the right side ...

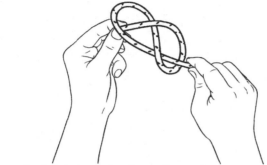

... and stick it into the loop from above.

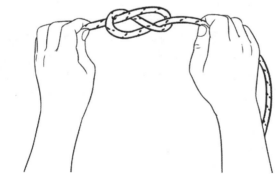

Now I pull both parts of the line, ...

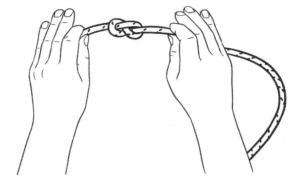

... and the figure-eight knot is finished.

For some of the nautical knots there are memory rhymes. For the figure-eight knot it reads as follows: There is a baby and I wrap a scarf around its neck. Then I put a dummy into its mouth. I pull on both ends of the line again and the figure-eight knot is finished.

Also, watch the video about how to tie the figure-eight knot on the Internet: *http://sailnator.com/figure-eight-knot/* and practice the figure-eight knot till you are able to tie it with closed eyes or/and behind your back.

Square Knot

In this chapter I show how to tie the square knot. We can attach two lines of the same strength with it. Follow these steps for tying the square knot:

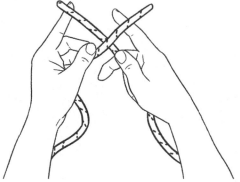

I start the same way as I would when tying a ribbon. I take both ends of the lines one above the other, ...

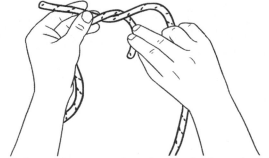

... and pull through one end underneath the other. For the next step it is now important which of the lines was lying on top of the other at the beginning.

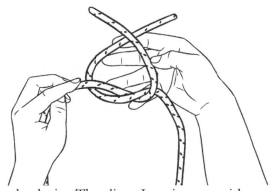

I just check it. The line I point at with my left forefinger was lying above at first.

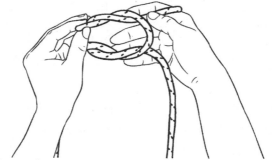

I take the end of it, put it over the other line again and wrap both lines around each other.

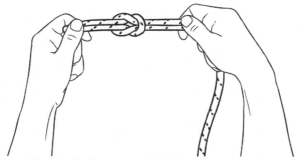

I now pull on all four parts of the lines at the same time and the square knot is finished.

The knot is tied right when both ends of the lines are on the same side. If not it is not the square knot. This one opens up easily.

It is even important that the line that was lying above first lies on top the second time too. We can open the square knot by holding one of the connected lines and pull the end that is parallel to it. That even works if the knot was pulled together very tight over some time.

Also, watch the video about how to tie the square knot on the Internet: *http://sailnator.com/square-knot/* and practice the square knot till you are able to tie it with closed eyes or/and behind your back.

Bowline Knot

In this chapter I show how to tie the bowline knot. We use the bowline knot to form a loop at the end of a line that does not contract. This is needed for example to fix a line at a mooring post or to attach the halyard on the head of a sail. Follow these steps for tying the bowline knot: Before I start it is useful to recognise which is the loose part and which the moored part of my line. Which end of my line would be attached somewhere in reality? For example at a cleat on my boat. So I tie a figure-eight knot in the end of my line to mark the moored part.

I place the figure-eight knot away from me over my left hand.

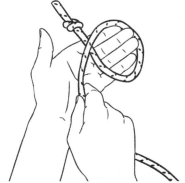

I take the loose part with my right hand and lay a loop where the loose part lies over the moored part of the line.

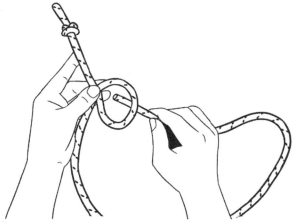

I take the point where the two parts cross between my thumb and my middle finger of my left hand. With my forefinger I keep the moored part at a distance.

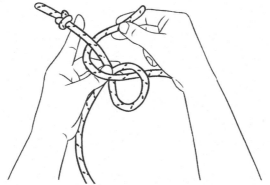

I take the loose part with the right hand now and stick it into the loop from underneath. Then I put it clockwise around the back of the moored part. I pull the loose part a little bit.

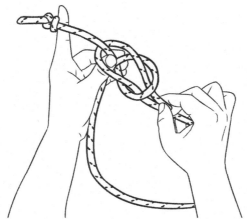

Now I stick the loose part into the loop again, but this time from above.

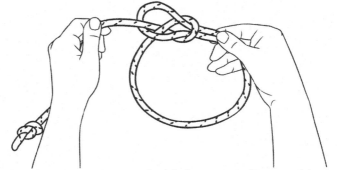

Now it is important to hold the moored part with the left hand and to pull with the right hand both bits of the loose part.

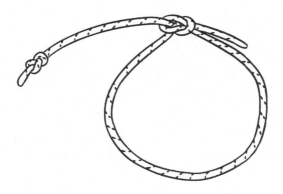

Now the bowline knot is finished.

When we put the loose part counter clockwise around the backside of the moored part the tail will be inside the loop afterwards. Then we can stick the loop better through a ring if necessary.

There is a memory rhyme for this knot too: Here I have a pond, out of the pond comes a (water-)snake, at the bank of the pond it goes clockwise around a tree and dives back into the pond on the other side. Now we pull the moored part and both bits of the loose part and the bowline knot is finished. If you do not like snakes you can let out a rabbit out of its hole that runs clockwise around a tree back into its hole again.

Also, watch the video about how to tie the bowline knot on the Internet: *http://sailnator.com/bowline-knot/* and practice the bowline knot till you are able to tie it with closed eyes or/and behind your back.

Cleat Knot

In this chapter I show how to tie the cleat knot. We use it to attach a line to a horn cleat. Follow these steps for tying the cleat knot:

Before I start I again tie a figure-eight knot in one end of the line. It shall represent my boat that I want to cleat on the jetty.

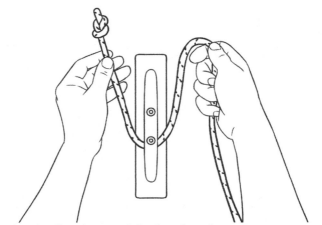

I take the line in my right hand and put it once around the base of the horn cleat.

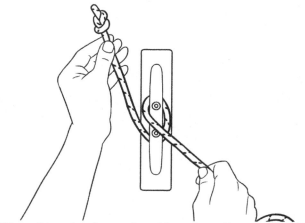

When I am back on the side where I started I lift the line and cross the cleat from the left to the right.

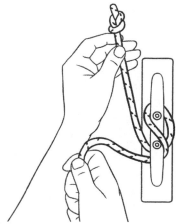

Then I pull the line through under the part of the cleat that is facing me.

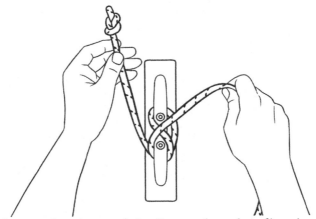

I cross the cleat and the line to the other direction and here comes the trick: Instead of again pulling through the line under the cleat I tie a loop which is called a bitter.

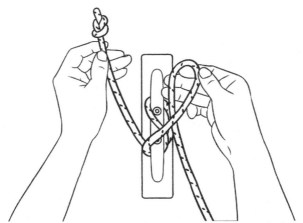

For that I take the tail between thumb and forefinger of the right hand and turn the line the way a loop appears where the loose part is under the moored part.

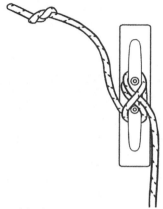

I put this loop over the part of the cleat that is away from me. The cleat knot is finished.

I memorize the progress like this: First I lay an O around the base of the cleat, than an X over it and then the bitter, a loop where the loose part is under the moored part. Then I put the bitter over the cleat. The cleat knot is finished.

O – X – Bitter

Also, watch the video about how to tie the cleat knot on the Internet: *http://sailnator.com/cleat-knot/* and practice the cleat knot till you are able to tie it with closed eyes. If you have no horn cleat just take your thumb and your forefinger and practice like that.

Clove Hitch

In this chapter I show how to tie the clove hitch. We use the clove hitch for example to attach a fender to the railing. Follow these steps for tying the clove hitch:

I tie a figure-eight knot in one end of my line that shall constitute the fender. The traversed line shall be a railing.

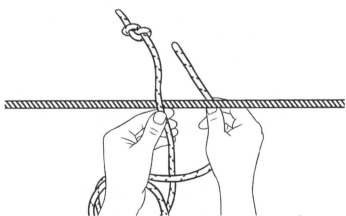

I lay the line over the railing that way the fender (the figure-eight-knot) hangs outside the boat. I now grab the loose part of the line with my right hand ...

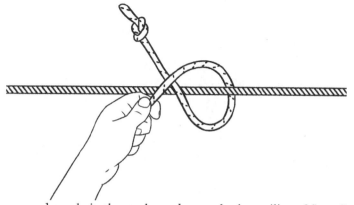

... and push it through underneath the railing. Now I grab the end of the line with my left hand from above and take it to my side of the railing by crossing the line that is hanging down.

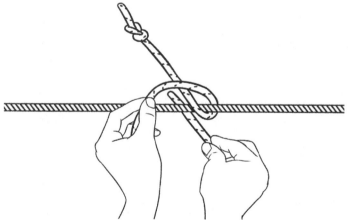

By doing this I leave a loop on the railing that I secure with the left hand.

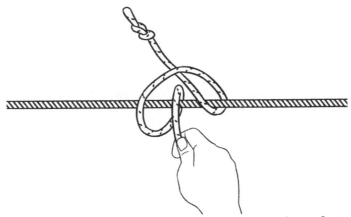

Now I stick the end of the line through this loop from below ...

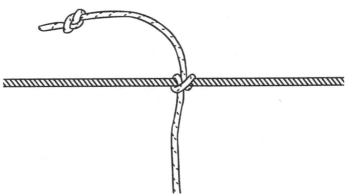

... and pull both parts of the line. Now the clove hitch is finished.

We can tie the clove hitch on slip too. Instead of the end of the line I push a bight underneath the crossing line. We can open the knot faster by tying it this way. But we have to anticipate losing the fender. Especially when the fender reaches the water surface and is hit by swell the knot might open by itself.

Also, watch the video about how to tie the clove hitch on the Internet: *http://sailnator.com/clove-hitch/* and practice the clove hitch till you are able to tie it with closed eyes.

Clove Hitch (laid)

In this chapter I show how to lay the clove hitch. We use the laid clove hitch when we want to put it over something. For example over a mooring post or if we want to secure the tiller with a line. Follow these steps to lay the clove hitch:

Again, I tie a figure-eight knot in one end of the line which marks the moored part of it.

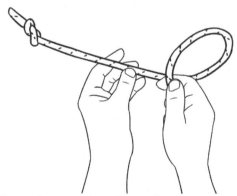

I lay a loop now where the loose part lies over the moored part ...

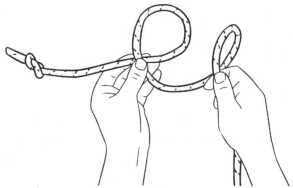

... and next to it a second loop ...

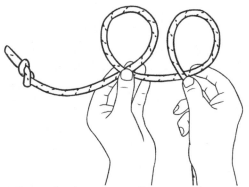

... where the loose part lies over the moored part.

I push the loop that is closer to the lines end, here the
right one, under the loop that is closer to the moored
end of the line.

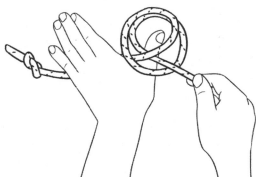

I put both loops that are lying one on the other over
my thumb, which serves as the post or the tiller.

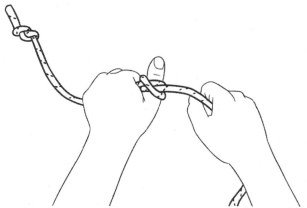

I pull on both parts of the line now and the laid clove hitch is finished.

Also, watch the video about how to lay the clove hitch on the Internet: *http://sailnator.com/clove-hitch-laid/* and practice the laid clove hitch till you are able to tie it with closed eyes.

Clove Hitch (thrown)

In this chapter I show how to throw the clove hitch. We use the thrown clove hitch for example when we want to attach a line on a mooring post quickly while keeping it under tension. Follow these steps to throw the clove hitch:

Again, I tie a figure-eight knot in one end of the line as the moored part. I imagine this is a boat that I want to moor to a post, which is represented by my left thumb in this case.

I place the moored part of the line along my left thumb ...

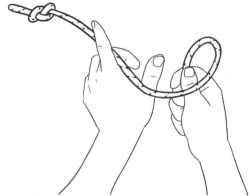

... and secure it with my left forefinger. I take the loose part of the line in my right hand. I turn the line into a loop where the moored part lies above the loose part of the line.

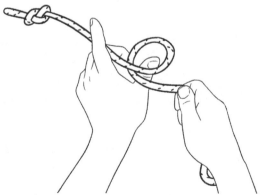

I put the loop over the post and pull the imaginary boat towards me as close as possible.

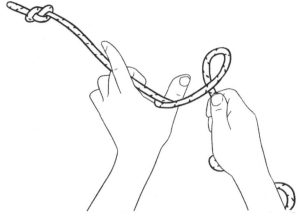

Now I lay a second loop the same way as the first one
...

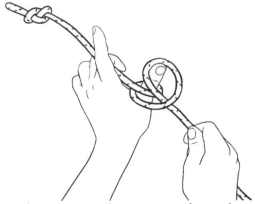

... and put it over the post too above the other loop.

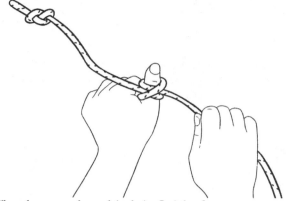

The thrown clove hitch is finished.

Also, watch the video about how to throw the clove hitch on the Internet: *http://sailnator.com/clove-hitch-thrown/* and practice the thrown clove hitch till you are able to tie it with closed eyes.

Sheet Bend

In this chapter I show how to tie the sheet bend. We use the sheet bend to connect two lines that are not the same strength. Follow these steps for tying the sheet bend:

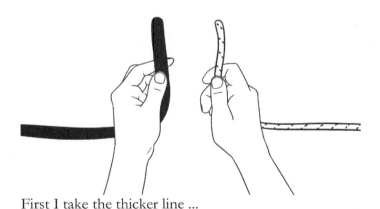

First I take the thicker line ...

... and design a so called bight at its very end. I hold
the bight between thumb and middle finger of my left
hand. Thereby the shorter part of the line points to
me.

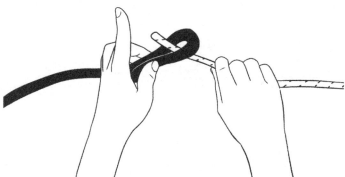

I take the thinner line with my right hand now and
push it through the bight from below.

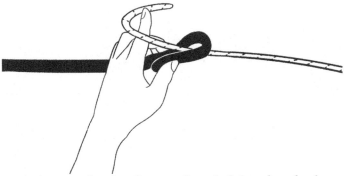

I put it over the forefinger of my left hand and release it.

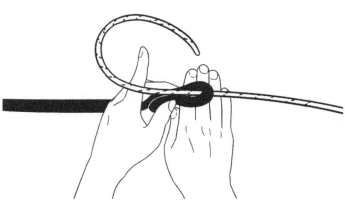

With my right hand I go through down the bight and pick up the thinner line.

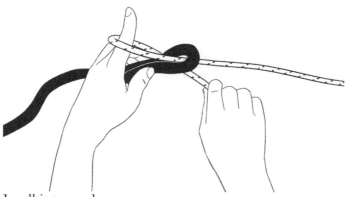

I pull it towards me ...

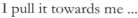

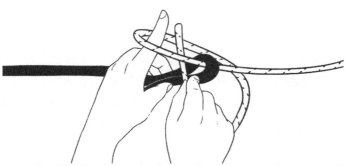

... and stick it through from the front under my left forefinger and left of the part of the thinner line that is already there. Then I release it again.

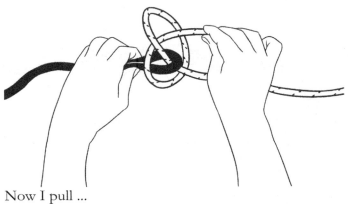

Now I pull ...

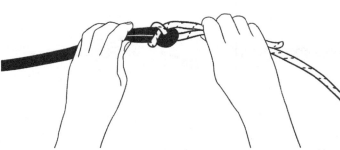

... all four parts of the lines at the same time. The sheet bend is finished.

We can also tie the sheet bend on slip. That way we can untie it quickly. I start the same way as with the normal sheet bend. I design a bight, stick the thinner line through and lay it over the forefinger. Now I design a bight in the thinner line as well and push it under the left forefinger.

I secure the new bight with the forefinger and I pull at the longer part of the thinner line. If I pull at the tail the knot opens up immediately.

Also, watch the video about how to tie the sheet bend on the Internet: *http://sailnator.com/sheet-bend/* and practice the sheet bend till you are able to tie it with closed eyes or/and behind your back.

Double Sheet Bend

In this chapter I show how to tie the double sheet bend. The double sheet bend unbolts not so easily because it is safer than the single sheet bend. But it also connects two lines that are not the same size. Follow these steps for tying the double sheet bend:

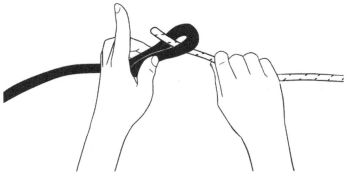

I start the same way as for the single sheet bend. I take the bight on the end of the thicker line between thumb and middle finger of the left hand.

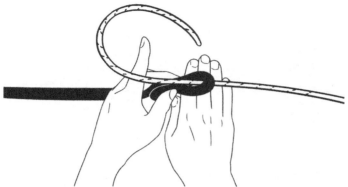

I stick the thinner line through the bight from below. I put it over the forefinger of my left hand. With my right hand I pick up the thinner line ...

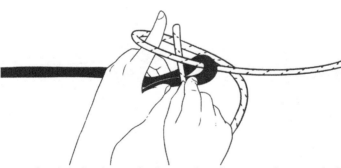

... and stick it through from the front under my left forefinger and left of the part of the thinner line that is already there.

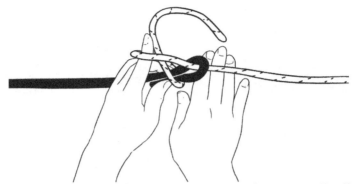

With the single sheet bend I would now pull all
together. But this time I go through under the bight
with my right hand and pick up the thinner line again.
I pull it towards me ...

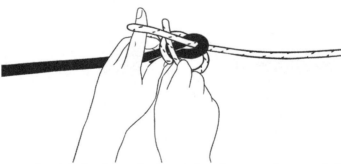

... and stick it through from the front under my left
forefinger again. The second time the line lies parallel
next to the first turn.

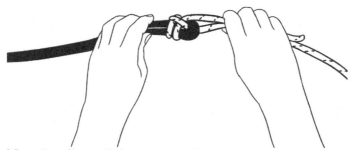

Now I pull on all four parts of the lines and the double sheet bend is finished.

We can tie the double sheet bend also on slip. Instead of the end of the line I stick again a bight under my left forefinger and pull all together. When the line has been pulled for a very long time, for example by towing a boat, it is much easier to untie the knot this way.

Also, watch the video about how to tie the double sheet bend on the Internet: *http://sailnator.com/double-sheet-bend/* and practice the double sheet bend till you are able to tie it with closed eyes or/and behind your back.

Round Turn
and two half Hitches

In this chapter I show how to tie one and a half round turns and two half hitches. We use the round turn and two half hitches for example to attach a line to a ring or a grommet. Follow these steps for tying the round turn and two half hitches:

Again, I tie a figure-eight knot in the end of the moored part of the line. I imagine that this is a boat that I want to attach on a ring. The ring is represented by the transverse line.

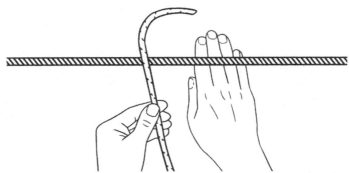

Now I put the loose part of my line over the transverse line. With my right hand I grab below the transverse line ...

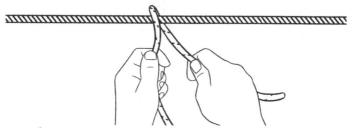

... and wrap the line ...

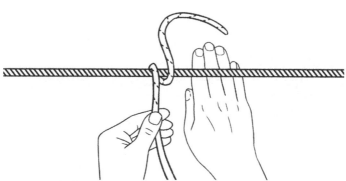

... around the transverse line once again. That are one and a half round turns now. I wrapped the line one and a half times around the transverse line.

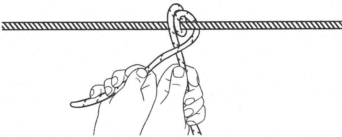

I take the loose part below the transverse line with my
right hand and put it above the moored part of the
line. That gives me a loop between the moored and the
loose part of the line.

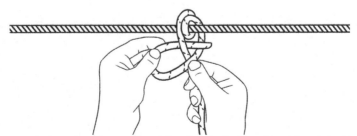

Now I take the tail with the left hand and stick it
through the loop from below.

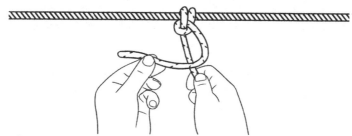

Then I cross the moored part once again with the loose part from top right to bottom left and again leave a loop.

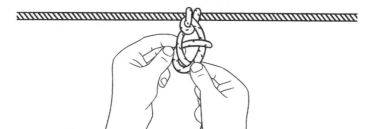

With the loose part I go underneath the moored part and stick the tail through the loop.

Now the round turn and two half hitches is finished.

It is very important to perform the two half hitches exactly the described way. As you see two parallel lines have to be crossed by one line. It results in a clove hitch on the moored part. If we do not perform the two half hitches the same way there are the two lines again. But they are not crossed now. The line that secures the knot lies transverse on them. This knot unties itself when the line sways to and fro.

Also, watch the video about how to tie the one and a half round turns and two half hitches on the Internet: *http://sailnator.com/round-turn-and-two-half-hitches/* and practice the round turn and two half hitches till you are able to tie it with closed eyes.

It is a good exercise to tie a bowline knot on one end of your line and imagine this is the ring. Then you tie a round turn and two half hitches with the other end of the line on it.

Rolling Hitch

In this chapter I show how to tie the rolling hitch. We use the rolling hitch for example if we want to attach a line to another line that is tensed. For example when several boats are supposed to be towed with one single line. It is possible to shift the knot on the line in one direction and to the other direction it stops. Follow these steps for tying the rolling hitch:

Again, I tie a figure-eight knot in the end of my line and imagine it is a boat that has to be towed. Before I start I think about in which direction the boat will be towed and from which direction the tension on the line comes from.

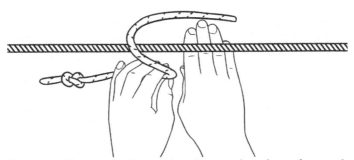

I put my line over the towing line and grab underneath the towing line with my right hand.

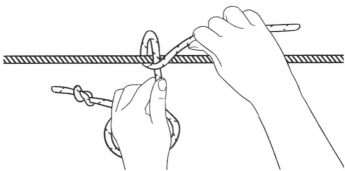

I take the end of the line up towards me and cross my line in the direction that the boat will be towed to. When the boat will be towed to the right, ...

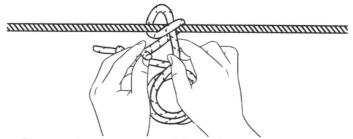

... I cross the line to the right. When the boat will be towed to the left, I cross the line to the left. I assume now that the boat will be towed to the right side and cross the line in this direction.

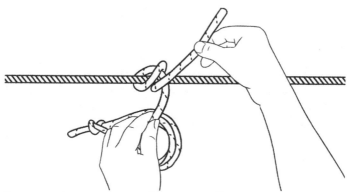

I repeat the process and wrap my line around a second time.

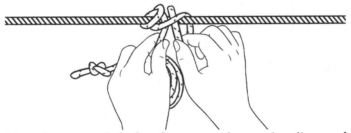

Now I put my left forefinger on the towing line and wrap it so that if I pull it back a loop emerges. I stick the end of the line directly through this loop, without wrapping the other part of the line again.

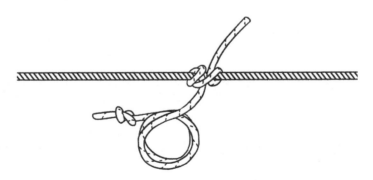

The rolling hitch is finished.

I can now move the knot to one direction on the towing line. To the other direction the two turns stop the line.

Also, watch the video about how to tie the rolling hitch on the Internet: *http://sailnator.com/rolling-hitch/* and practice the rolling hitch till you are able to tie it with closed eyes.

Cleat with Bowline Knot

In this chapter I show how to attach a line to a horn
cleat with a bowline knot. If we, for example, want to
put a line around a mooring post on slip back to the
same cleat it is often difficult to use the horn cleat for
two cleat knots. The cleat might be too small for it.
Especially when the line is a thick mooring line.
Follow these steps to attach a line to a horn cleat with
a bowline knot:

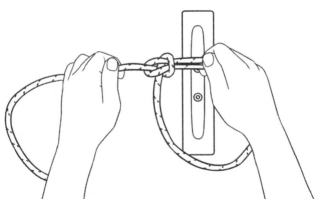

I tie a bowline knot in the very end of my line with a
relatively big loop.

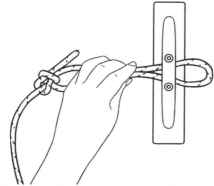

I place the loop from the side where the line should run to later into the base of the cleat almost till the knot is reached.

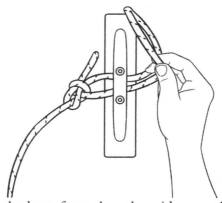

Now I put the loop from the other side over the upper

...

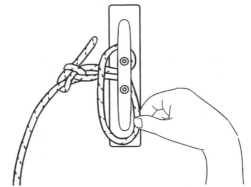

... and the lower horn of the cleat.

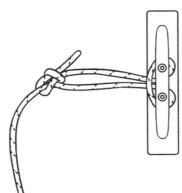

Now the line is attached to the cleat. But it is only safe when it is under tension.

I now can lay the line around a mooring post and tie it with the cleat knot the second time without building up a big bunch of knots. The disadvantage when doing it that way is that the length of the line cannot be changed anymore. And if there is tension on the line it is very hard to untie the knot.

Also, watch the video about how to attach a line to a horn cleat with a bowline knot on the Internet: *http://sailnator.com/cleat-with-bowline-knot/*

Appendix

More books by Alexander Meyer:

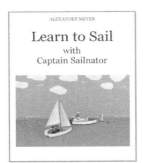

Learn to Sail with Captain Sailnator

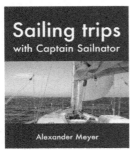

Sailing trips with Captain Sailnator

All books are also available as ebooks.

Made in the USA
Coppell, TX
30 March 2022

75774009R00033